DEAREST WATER

DEAREST WATER

POEMS BY NANCY TAKACS

MAYAPPLE PRESS 2022

Published by   Mayapple Press
               362 Chestnut Hill Road
               Woodstock, NY 12498
               mayapplepress.com

ISBN 978-952781-09-41
Library of Congress Control Number: 2021952225

ACKNOWLEDGEMENTS

Many thanks to the editors of the following poetry journals
for publishing these poems, some with different titles, and in
slightly different forms: *2River Review, American Journal of
Poetry, Canary, Clover, Hayden's Ferry Review, Helper Project's
American Crossroads Art Exhibit, Kestrel, Limberlost Review,
Mapping Literary Utah, Missouri Review, Moon City Review, On
the Seawall, Pushcart Prize Anthology 2020, Red Rock Review,
Terrain.org, Weber: a Journal of the Contemporary West, West
Texas Literary Review, Wild Animals* (Outlaw Artists Press, 2008).

Special thanks to the wise and helpful friends who gave me their
thoughts on this book in its earlier form: Linda Heuring, Kate
Kingston, Thomas Murtha, Book Cliff Poets, and The Mayapple
Writers' Group. And to poets Star Coulbrooke, Sally Rosen
Kindred, and Derek Sheffield, for their very kind words. Much
gratitude to Judith Kerman, poet and editor of Mayapple Press,
for her generosity and hard work in editing, designing, and
making this book. Thanks to Judith Buckwalter, amazing artist,
for sharing your gorgeous image *The Journey Home* for the cover.
Love to my wonderful family for your encouragement always.
And to my husband, Jan Minich, for your intelligence, gentleness,
and love.

Cover art by Julia Buckwalter. Author photo by Jan Minich. Book
design and layout by Judith Kerman in Constantia with titles in
Notram.

CONTENTS

for Jan, Ian, and Jenni

1. POEMS FOR WOMEN ONLY

FOR WOMEN ONLY

It wasn't easy inventing the language,
turning our *mmm's* and *ahh's*
into hummingbirds and gardens.
It wasn't easy grinding the corn,
beading the slippers,
baking over those open fires.

Maybe that's why our mothers
forgot their ironing, their
embroidering of swans
on towels, left pans
to sit overnight
on the stove. That's when
we women invented
the dishwasher, invented
the words for summer afternoon
in the backyard, reading
The Smithsonian instead of
House Beautiful.

My mothers and I went on
to invent many gardens,
rambling roses, apple trees.
We fluttered in the honeysuckle
trailing our green wings behind us.

We invented the hibachi,
rice salad with raisins and almonds,
lightly done salmon in lemon
with a hint of parsley.

We ate outside listening
to the sparrows and chickadees,
on our glass table that shattered
once when lightning struck it.

It was then we invented
the portable table,
sprang it open near lakes

where we swam the butterfly
to the deep, and back a couple of times.

We ate pastrami
and tiramisu from the deli,

opened our journals,
uncapped our fine-point pens
under the tang of pines.

after Tony Hoagland

REMNANTS

Some Saturdays,
after saying our rosaries at early Mass,
Aunt Ginny and I took the hour-long
bus ride to Manhattan's garment district.

I'd help her sort
through messy bins, pick out
a yard or two of paisley challis,
a piece of shimmering shantung
she found alluring.

Single, prim, devout,
she was so good
at her own designs
and invisible seams
she became loose with pleasure
as our palms felt the prickles
of weave, our wrists the feather
of selvage.

Over our arms
we hung watered silks
and sheer chiffons
she would conjure
into blouses for herself,
my mother, and me.

That was where
I learned about luxury
for almost nothing, how to eye
the sharp store owner,
and bargain bitterly
for whatever I love.

Spell to Banish a Ghost

At night I hear Anna
snipping toenails
in my wicker chair,
smell her cologne,
Ambush.

Once my favorite aunt,
she whispered to me
with venom
when I was twenty
she never liked me
because I was born
last in our family
and took her place.

She died alone
last October
with a brain tumor.

She eyes me in sink water
from my mother's dishes,
her blue face in their lilies,
her earrings like onions.

She cocks her head,
skinny robin on my side-mirror,
then craps on my door handle.

So tonight on this quarter moon,
I make a fire.
I find my red frying pan,
fill it with lavender oil
and wait till it hisses.

I hold my only picture of her,
write her name on the back of it,
and kiss it three times.

NAILS FOR THE NEW YEAR

Aubrey spins me a circle
of white gel powder
and sparks of ruby.

My old friend opens the door
and sits down with Kathy
to sift bottles
for the perfect blue.

We parted ways four years ago
over her betrayal,
a lie about me to a friend.
She apologized.
I've never called.

Both in the front window,
we're quiet as it snows,
then raise small questions.

Her timbre quavers.
Her cheeks have new
contours. She asks
for my new number.

We have to turn away
for the women
to hold our hands still.

Such small canvases we are
as they wipe away slivers
from any cuticle
that weeps,

asking us if we want roses
or jewels, heads down
as they stir shiny filaments
to embellish us for the new year
with the finest brush.

Making Up

is like the first pickle from a mason jar,
raspberry jam in the tapioca. My husband
speaks to me for the first time after our
argument that shimmered with hooves.
Now his voice is all hallowed and velour.
Now my voice is hazy and mango. We halt
our sorrows for now. We go out to the tulips
and have a cookie. I put on my magenta
sweatshirt. The dusky sky has one tamp of bitter.
Holding a hand can be like a hornet in a balloon.
It takes two hours for our toes to get drowsy.

FOSSIL FISH

Two fish on a slab,
each an eye-shape
with the half-shine
of a fingernail
over blue spines,
faces pointed
in the life that has
become them,
harbored in mud they
couldn't swim out of,
sideways in the last
of that warm sea
dried up a million
years ago. If my
mother were alive
and here with me,
she would think
of the inlet where
she and my father
brought a bucket
of killies, some days
they baited their lines,
and never argued.

ACCIDENT

A neighbor doesn't know I can see him peeing
on his pyre of burning leaves.

My insurance agent most likely
won't pick up her phone until noon.

I'm wondering if I should leave the corduroy
of this couch, and walk the mile
for a double espresso.

Or pat myself
on the back like the yoga teacher
says we should do, after our hardest pose.

The brilliant yellow trees say: *Alive, Alive.*

Maybe I shouldn't care my old red car
is smashed into another world.

I've never seen this bird here—a Steller's jay
insisting something I should take to heart,
his yakking and yakking salty-sweet.

I take from the cracked bowl this ripe peach,
lift it to my face in rapture, then float back
into my body.

I think I'll stay in the house all day
and read poetry from a time
when people rowed out in little boats.

THE BEEKEEPER

for Karen

My friend keeps bees.
They rise around her,
alighting on her veils.

When she lost her mother,
she left the armature
she had curved into the figure
of a young woman
cradling a bird.

As the bees swarm
in her long garden,
she watches to see what they will do.

As a sculptor she has learned
so much from her hands,
so much from her body.
Now she learns from her bees.

~

This is spring
when all the decisions are made.

The bees are ready among
the lavender, the carnations,
making room for another queen,
feeding her the royal jelly.

Who will mate with her?
Who will see the mating flight?

The ones in the hive beat their wings,
an updraft of pheromones
to lead her back home.

~

My friend sees how the bees organize,
work quickly, brush in and out of
every hyacinth and violet,
every blossom of her plum tree.

She brushes honey on her toast,
swirls drops in her lavender flan.
She is in love with the work
that has come from flowers,
from the delicate legs
that carry baskets of pollen
at dusk to their secret place.

She is careful
not to walk between the beelines
from heather to the hives.

~

She sees how bees sculpt hexagons,
the most efficient shapes
to harbor their labor,
how they sweeten just for the hive,
how easily they accept dying.

~

She watches the drifts
of them, in and out,
and is gentled by them.

She is always careful
not to interrupt the queen.

~

Grief goes out to pasture.

~

She paints a woman,
an orchestra conductor
pulling streams of air from horns and violins,
the woman's eyes wide open.

Burgundies and blues
in the veins and bones
of the woman's hands,
violet fury in her hair.

~

She has learned the word *let,*
the word *inter,*

leaves the bees more
than enough honey for winter,

and takes up the armature again,
remakes the tired arms, smooths
the lowered neck of the girl
who has been all along cradling the bird
in her light-filled studio.

~

The new queen is ready.

If you spend a life watching bees,
you might never see her fly.

AUGUST, NORTH WOODS

The toxic tang of tobacco. The medicine taste
of sassafras tea. Just a couple of tomatoes
above their fungal yellow leaves.
And the last long phlox lies down.
My wild days will never end.
The bees still come to the milkweed.
The phoebes surge in the goldenrod.

A young mother and I chat while I'm a judge
for the sand castle contest. Her little girl looks up
at me with her wide face and teal eyes.
She's three, named Evie, sculpts an alligator
and places a pine cone on its head.

AMETHYSTS

My neighbor Diane wears them
on her fingers, wrists, and neck
to heal from last year's stroke,
her spring mastectomy,
now her broken leg.

She crutches out with me
to the Delta Diner, where they serve
the best perch in Wisconsin.
She turns her rings
as we talk and wait for Emma,
the young server who *oohs* and *ahhs*
over Diane's bracelet.

Once a union negotiator,
Diane flew the world,
working her charm. I can feel it now
as she grins and says I'm her favorite poet.

I like the word amethyst in my mouth,
its double diagraths, consonants
that feel like a wish with a thorn.

She tells me the name comes from *amestusthos*
meaning sober, balancing the gambler,
the shopper, the alcoholic,

and winks: *I'm a good witch,*
careful with my amethysts. I drink
two glasses of wine each day at six.

Diane takes my unadorned hand, says
Love, someday I'll bring you an amethyst.

We slow-walk to my car, then drive
the long way home, past virgin forests,
and open miles of blazing maple and aspen.
She opens her window and calls:
Merlot! Citron! Cinnamon!
Gamboge! Eau de Nil!

UTAH GARDEN

Hollyhocks rise
with their sturdy skirts,
like the women who grow up
in this desert town,
not meaning to go anywhere
but where they must,
impossible to uproot.

Mother-of-thyme
creeps on. Sage holds one
blue leaf. Chives thicken.
I never liked them, but I gather
their violet-scented flowers.

My prickly fronds and pods
of poppies are the ones raising hell
in the stubble
along my chain link.

I rake sorrel and thistle
away from their maze,

for the coming rain,
their flaming crepe,

their centers dark
and alive as bees.

Coconut Oil

Twist the jar's gold lid and open.
Let the tropics come to you
for your lazy afternoon's *toilette*.

~

Suddenly you're fifteen with the scent,
slicking it over your pale thighs, too-big shoulders,
on the land-strip between your double-A-cup breasts,
to transform the body you did not love,
on the sacred beach in Belmar, New Jersey.

But it was the body you trusted
in the icy waves as they churned you
till you emerged clean and salty,
ready to oil yourself again, needing to burn,
peel your skin away to its heart.

~

Dip your fingers now
into the jar, and scoop
the organic balm into
your cabin's snowed-in air.

Circle it over your shoulders,
massage gently
around moles at your nape.
Butter your breasts.
your nipples,
smooth your belly fold,
your C-section scar,
your muscled thighs.

Fragrant and shining,
close your flannel robe,
keep the scent
of piña colada,
cream pie,
Almond Joy
all winter night.

I Still Have a Voice

Why do I wait to separate jewelry
that lives in tangled knots,
till I want my lucky peridot necklace?

When I wear it, I feel like Joni Mitchell again,
belting out *Ladies of the Canyon*
so my *Don't Tread on Me* neighbor can hear.

Always in the background, my 6th grade voice
tolled the alto for funeral Masses,
or hummed *stream* in a 3-woman chorus
in *Climb Every Mountain,* until I took up
guitar after my boyfriend, golden-haired
James, plucked his twangy 12-string
and I fell in love with the way he sang *Wild Horses,*
and knew it was for me.

Finding myself solo, trilling Joni's silver notes in *Blue,*
I wrote songs to perform with Maryann
on our college radio, lambasting the Vietnam war,
until her father called the station and had
the tape destroyed.

So I open my jewelry box
that smells of tarnished silver and my
aunt's gardenia-scented powder. She died
without singing much, left me her ring,
a turquoise necklace, and lots of chains.

I should untangle those chains,
maybe turn them in for cash. I could use
a nice set of watercolors, swish
crimson, gold-green, ultramarine
with lots of water on the page, and watch
a figure emerge from the drift,
like the spooky head of a parrot,
or a fish that flips its body in a pink dusk.

I slip my guitar under my breast again
and blue my voice, not quite having Joni's
verve and range, and beauty, but I'm glad
I still have it, can still wing *A Case of You*:

Oh, you're in my blood like holy wine.
You taste so bitter and so sweet.
Oh, I could drink a case of you, darling.
Still I'd be on my feet. I would still be on my feet,
wearing my peridot necklace, making chords swim
over my craggy picking, feeling this music
more luminous than my aunt's star sapphire,
more like sudden watercolor pines, while my own
new song is feathering out from the wet paper.

RESURFACING

Reclaiming my son's red room
after he moves away from home,
lingering over the many colors of white,
Trillium, Ghost, Dove's Wing, Snow—
I pick Porpoise for my walls,
Lightning Bolt for my door.
I fill holes with fresh plaster,
roll the room into lightness.

I hang my friend's painting
of an exuberant woman,
her hair woven in poppies,
tossing an empty laundry basket
into a turquoise sky,

then sit in my mother's
maple chair, rest my heels
on its rungs, remembering
in this chair she told me my father
would divorce her if she didn't
agree to have another child.

She believed in sex only for procreation,
and didn't want another child,
but gave in, said I was created
from ten quick ejaculations.

Maybe that's why I want to put
my coffee cup down on the table's veneer,
not on the coaster she gave me,
a cinnamon owl with obsidian eyes.

I redo her antique cupboard,
paint the outside Coastal Blue,
the inside Rainy Lavender.
empty my ashtray, think
I will give up smoking, light
the lemongrass essence.

I line up my poems, take time
to organize, turn pages all afternoon
in my new cushy chair
called The Womb,

think how I almost didn't live
except for my father's insistence,
his penis on hold for nine years
between me and my brother,
remember my mother's words:
You were worth it.

Cranking my table that adjusts
to acute angles, for painting watercolors,
the kind that start with thick paper
in a warm bath, I stab and swirl
my brushes in Forest, Viridian, Spring,
letting them bleed new leaves
that wander into a desert April,
drift and burst into stars.

This is the first layer.
My next will let Alizarin Crimson
bloom in the sky.

2. WILDNESS

WOLVERINE,

Each time I go to the mountain
I think you'll appear to me
in your shaggy coat
with the sheen of silver
and your tell-tale ivory stripe.
But you're smarter than I am.
I'm kind of a loner like you, skunk-bear,
but way too soft, lounging
on my futon with a paperback
on my breast, digesting tasty
memories of Proust. Though
I might write a poem beginning
with a snarl that ripples from
my ribcage to my fingernails
to the page, it gnaws for a long time
before I can say it out loud.
I play your growls and huffs
on my laptop as you swallow,
your victory language,
while I gamble on virtual slots
and lose, simmering my chicken
with two tablespoons of sage.
Wolverine, I've leaned
into creeks for watercress,
picked the raspberries
bears have been in,
looked into the eyes
of great-horned owls,
glimpsed the bear, the fox.
And fed some. Terrible, I know.
I should have let the wild be wild.
Humans call *you* terrible,
caribou-hound, bone-crusher,
tooth-eater. Trappers wait for you,
snowmobilers spin across your space.
I hope you're still running and running,
hunting and hunting somewhere
wide and cold enough for you,
gulo-gulo, one long stanza in the body
of your breath.

EATING AT THE PIER

A scallop has two hundred eyes, and here I am
sticking a fork into one, my tongue

running over the soft groove where the cook
pulled the ligament, as I eye the serene green

backs of the Apostle Islands, hear what sounds like
a whooping crane. Some of us have guided cranes

with an ultralight a thousand miles back to their nests.
Sometimes we can be earnest in saving animals,

for even one to have babies. We recognize wildness
though not usually in ourselves. There are no verses

here for man or woman who's boiled a live lobster.
Tonight the sky is so clear it will soon be irised with stars,

and we'll immediately think of heaven, of eyes.
We're civilized. Eyes watch us from the sky,

the tanks, the deep. I swallow another scallop,
maybe the last eyes I will ever eat.

SWEATER

It's feeling a little chilly this August
as I watch for the hummingbird
who drinks from my fuchsia.

A wolf howled twice last night,
and it seemed like she was announcing
the coming of fall as I ate the last peach.

I've tinted virgin wool with tansy and lupine,
learning this from a neighbor. The yarns
turned soft yellow, violet-blue.

But there will never be a next time. I feel
guilty for wanting to knit wool. So many
bad things done to the sheep, treated

so roughly, only as commodities,
some left with wounds where flies
lay their eggs, maggots eat their

flesh from inside. And then wolves
are shot anywhere near them, even
miles from their pens. So many animals

people hate, or love in our bellies,
or for warming our backs with a sweater.
This summer I was chased by a grouse,

stung by wasps, met a bear, and after,
couldn't decide if I felt more, or less, human.
I'll hoof my old bucket to the dump

for recycling, stuff my wool in a basket
and close the lid. I may never hear
a wolf again.

STOLEN

The clasp on a coral-and-silver necklace
I stole once, still prickles like I just got a haircut.

I went to Confession.
But I never took it back.

This morning, my coral trumpet-vine beams me
to a sandstone tower in the Utah desert

where beige stones blush over sea-green.
Where little shells once held antediluvian animals.

Where the primitive looks for us again.
The desert can haunt anyone with its dune music.

But it's the call of the chickadee, who keeps
pronouncing its name, that makes me think

we humans are infamous, wanting to be famous.
We're frantic to nicker, begging

for a little kindness, stealing what we can
to show it off on our granite countertops.

Not enough are we guttural, or loving.
So we steal a silver tongue, like the chickadee's,

its root beer song, its syllables that
rhyme over and over with *me.*

THE GARDEN STATE

I keep an artificial hydrangea in my vase,
its pale blue shot-through with khaki.

In Jersey, we called them snowballs,
so much fuller than roses, so weirdly azure

with an under-shine of rust. Kind of like
my childhood New Jersey

still called the Garden State, despite
its constant rise of lobster houses

and glitzy hotels down the Shore,
pricy beaches that used to be free

thirty years ago when my parents and I
drove from our city, to buoy ourselves in the swells,

churned in sand under each cool wave
until our lips turned blue.

~

I'm beginning to like the idea of a permanent
flower—its harlequin petals,

that one eye watching me,
viridian leaves always pointed towards heaven—

maybe because of what I've lost—
all the wonder if milkweed just now gone

to seed here in Wisconsin,
Monarchs' chrysalides blown open

by new wings rushing to Canada.
How easily mothers and fathers die,

leaving their offspring to keep their kind alive.
It's a miracle. Like memory can be,

how even my silk hydrangea
can usher me back to our garden's snowballs

I'd get lost under for a long time,
their hide-and-seek lushness and quiet fragrance,

their trove of insects I would cup and touch,
place black in their tawny blue blossoms,

my mother always knowing where I was
as she eased open the window screen,

pinning our swimsuits on the line,
not yet calling me in for supper.

ICE

Minocqua, Wisconsin

On Lake Avenue, we tourists lick ice
cream, bobbing our heads. Locals call us
cone-faces. They live in Mexico all winter
on what they make on us summers. A cool

August. Mobs in the thrift store for cheap
shirts, maybe something bizarre for the
Pirate's Ball. Waiting for his wife, a man
holds a Coke, jiggling the cubes around.

At his feet old ice skates, behind his shoulders
unwanted pink and yellow glass pitchers,
as he sits on a white vinyl-and-metal chair
like the ones my mother had in our kitchen.

She made ice all summer, upending aluminum
trays into those pitchers of Kool-Aid—Strawberry,
Lemon-Lime, Ice-Blue—and doubling the sugar.
We never thought about glaciers melting

or that ICE would become an acronym for
displacement, for cruelty. *This shallow lake here
freezes easy in December,* the talkative store owner
tells me, and that the oldest woman in Minocqua

cleats across it till spring, earrings dangling
beneath her earmuffs, to talk politics, telling
others over their sausage gravy that climate
change is on our doorsteps, and how ICE

is using our taxpayer money to deport
all the good people in cities—
restaurant owners, nurses, neighbors,
putting them on planes when they've been here

for twenty years, without a crime. He asks
what I think. I say: *I love this woman.*
My mother and I back then couldn't have
imagined what the world has become. In Jersey

hurricanes came and went. The weather
was mostly pleasant. We welcomed our neighbors,
African-American, Korean, Puerto-Rican.
Summer nights our mothers would unfold

beach chairs and sit on each other's porches,
watching each other's children, treating
every child as their own, stirring sugar and ice
into the Kool-Aid, pouring us cup after cup.

WILD ANIMALS

I'm up early to make the yoga
class by the lake.

But I have to keep my cats in—
I saw a fisher around last night.

At the prison where I taught
I forget the guard's face
but not the weeping ones
of my poetry students
who told me they hurt people once
and begged me for criticism.

Poetry was almost as good
as the cats they secretly fed.

I was only locked up once,
in a closet, by a nun in second grade
when I couldn't stop laughing with a friend.

My prison friends tried to send me
letters and poems after I left,
but the warden wouldn't allow it.
He explained we were getting too close
and had to protect me, but the real reason
was that townies near the prison
complained about inmates
getting college credit.

My husband asked me if in college
I ever partied all night to see the sunrise.
I said I didn't stay out much,
I had to work early. I called
the cops once on a crowd singing
at 3 a.m. Living where I did,
I never drove the hour beyond
neighborhoods just to see the sun
squint behind skyscrapers.

Now the sun sneaks up
over this meadow to make it brilliant.

Yesterday a letter squeaked through:
one of my inmates sent a new poem
He's allowed to grow wildflowers now.
He's in charge of a sweat lodge.
He has another cat.

One of my cats is scratching the glass door
but I'm afraid to let her go
to the woods this early.

I wish I could let her, this calico
who has often bitten me,
often lain with me, eye to eye.

My cousin worked at a zoo
and befriended the oldest lion,
gentle at his age, who even
put his head on her lap
and let her stroke his mane.
The lion gave her happiness.
She said she gave the lion stability.
But she never let him out.

When I get to the lake, the yoga teacher
will ask us all to salute the sunrise.

Some people believe wild animals can't love.

Dearest Water,

In the searing heat of Dead Horse Point
looking over a vertical cliff,
I walk near the corral
where unwanted horses were
once left to die.

You have given us saliva
and this rim of crimson,

an altar cloth of air,
your distant promise.

Seeing your green curve
at the bottom
of this canyon,

they broke out
and leapt to their deaths.

My own thirst cruises like a lantern
over hoodoos and dry tides.

Your scent steams
like a live secret,

water,
my good memory.

I am thirsty
for the lost.

WHY I BECAME BLACK DRAGON CANYON

I needed the spit of crow wings,
a heron flapping in tree-pose on my shoulder,
a cougar on alert under my piñons.
I needed sun to scheme through my bodies,
the beige earth of my openings,
the wind to shear off bits of me,
then amethyst my bones.
I wanted to be carved out of aimlessness.
I needed my other side to finally
shadow me, shuck me, as I waited
in silence for the manna
of planets, the icy blossoms of stars.
I needed paintbrush and mallow
to whisk up through my toes.
I wanted a waterfall for grasses
to thicken, be green, then go gray
at my knees. I needed to let my faces
become varnished persimmon.
I wanted to drink rain
from my own stones.
I needed that juniper to brush me.

WILDNESS

Like you loved wildness,
I love the touch
of lead on the page
in a winter's litany of snowfalls.

Like you, I love the feel
of dough under my knuckles,
how it doubles up
when it works, gives
under pressure, lifts
cleanly from my board
when I roll up its tongue
of cinnamon-sugar.

Like you loved wildness,
I will not take Xanax.
I will keep up my teeth
for biting into apples,
keep the half-smile of my mother,
watch my pencil cast its red shadow
on my skin at the crux
of thumb and forefinger as I write
this poem to you at the Kona Grill
on the backs of old receipts
from my purse.

I'm eating a spicy fish taco
and oily fried rice, thinking about
trying a sake bomber
on my bamboo placemat
where it's just me and a gray-haired man
at the next table, who digs into
his beet salad, a song from Nine Inch Nails
piping outside under our awning
printed with palm trees.

I think you might prefer the sound
of Voodoo Rolls
and their description on my menu

in winged italics:
a cool tang of ginger
and a humble citrus,

as I look at your face
on this biography of you,
the only photo known to be you,
thinking how I know you
with your velvet necklace,
a book nearby, your hand
that has to touch a wildflower.

Emily, I wish my Monday
was a little like yours,
stopping at Sue's
with a coconut cake
for some gossip
and a sneak of brandy,

not searching to find the counter
for anti-aging cream, or worrying about
a ringtone in a restaurant,
or spilling hot sauce on wool.

You never wore
a skirt that had to be dry-cleaned.
You were wise with white cotton
for the ease, you said,
of throwing a dress in the washtub
among the bedsheets
with a cup of bluing.

Like you loved wildness,
I want to open the door,
close the door, refuse visitors,
and keep to my hand-written poems.

I think of how friends
carried your coffin lightly
through a field of buttercups,
and how someday I want to be buried
with violets and a lady's slipper,
and a poem from you.

Blue Universe

Name the sky a pale turquoise
behind the pencil lace of pitch black trees,
name this sculpture cerulean,
woman with a garnet heart, hair of piñon,
wiry antlers, fingertips of leaves. Name
the mountain lion opal blue, whose desert
becomes the City of the Future.
Name the black bear royal blue
as she looks down to a racket of hounds,
a gun. Watch early butterflies, small-blues,
skim the lavender froth of wild mustard
that is one day nothing, the next, streaming
through weed-yards, roadsides.
Inhale its musky breath. Watch desert clouds
trail off like denim work shirts of miners
in the dawn-blue, gathering for another
day of darkness, lungs spattered with dust.
Call this computer screen periwinkle,
then banish its clarity for earthy oxide
in the pigments of robins' eggs.

Listen to the jay's whisper song,
water notes like a call from childhood,
and the next-door shepherd's howl
before the train, azure in his throat.
See the sky go lighter on its way up
into the atmosphere, a casual blue
so light it's almost not there
over another Sunday with coffee,
plum blossoms, a drive to the desert,
and juniper berries whose gin
you rub behind your ear. Let this day
be just another that Earth tilts
on its axis, as you wait for the lazuli
buntings, who always arrive in May
to your feeder in their colors of Baja.

Believe the blue universe is what you live for,
need memory for, take up tools and draw
a new mandala for, sketch with colors
you desperately love more than anything,

a hyacinth so unforgettable, an iris so present,
they tattoo your palm. Name the branches
of ink in your veins as you say *my day is done,*
as the world comes down on all of us,
and we feel it as it falls, looking at dusk,
the wane of its violet, the light we felt
all day on our shoulders, our packs,
our arms, and our hair. Turn to the holy indigo
of night that remembers us to the owl
and the coyote, the raccoon and the nighthawk,
midnight that will piece us whole again,
with these wishes we carry, each of us in our orbit
before the light comes back to us and we rise.

3. INVISIBLE JEWELS

ODE TO DILL

Lush with syllables
in your starry umbels,

you hold a séance
in my kitchen each September.

How can I forget
your wake in the pickles,

your alto voice
between the potato,
tomato?

O, dill for my salmon,
dill for my soup,

in my mother's garden
you spoke
beyond the roses,

spilled seed
into our hushed palms,

brushed your mermaid hair
against our shoulders.

WHAT MY DOG KNOWS

is how the smell of shampoo
means I'm going out,
and the blow dryer
means without her.

She still asks
with her butterfly ears
wide open.

She is pine-scented
from yesterday's bath,
brushed, ready
to go if I want her,

trot to the lake and roll
in something rotten
as soon as I turn my back.

She's small but loves to bark
at all the big dogs in the park,
slip her collar
and lunge for their throats.

If I would only
take her,
and let her.

WHEN I'M ALONE

I wake up wanting
peach-and-pecan muffins
with a dash of chili.

Too lazy, I eat a bagel,
blend what I saved
for a stir fry:
celery, kale, watercress,
and swill it from a beer glass.

I slip unpaid bills
under the Eiffel Tower paperweight
a Saginaw poet once gave me
because she said a rock
cracking my windshield
wasn't a good welcome to Michigan,

then lie down in the middle
of the upstairs rug
and breathe,
doing the Child's Pose,
or legs-up-the-wall,
and think about meditating
but don't.

I squeeze a rubber ball
with my right hand,
strengthen it to open
the pickle jar,

open books already read
but almost forgotten,
and take to heart Emerson's line:
*Moons are no more
bounds to spiritual powers than bat balls,*

and notice the moon dangling
from a branch, like a lost earring.

WHAT DOES THE DAY SAY?

It says, take that coral shirt
from the back of your closet,

find Humbug Canyon
where you can dangle
your feet over a ledge,

look down into layers
and islands of rock
the colors of wine in sunlight.

Or you could make a kale-and-berry
smoothie, then gorge yourself
at the taco stand
just a block away,
on tamales rolled fresh in corn leaf.

The day says it is still dark
but the light will always come to you.

It promises you will learn more
about the Peony Star,
eat the last nasturtiums,
and offer a muffin
to the horse in the field behind you.

It adds, there are clothes
to be sorted, money
mailed to Verizon,
as you close the laptop,
let it sleep.

It barks,
let's start a revolution,
it's not too late
to help the climate.
It sighs, watch this hurricane.
It promises a flash flood.

It believes more cups of green tea
will save us, more
avocados.

It lets the scent of sweat
take you back to the streets
where you marched to protest,
expecting your body to count.

MEDITATION

I don't know the answer to plastic.
Or why I can never find the lids
to my glass bowls. Don't know why
my roses won't grow near pine,
and my hydrangea looks good
only every other year.

I don't know why
kosher salt makes a gentler brine,
a white-chestnut leaf
looks like it has bad handwriting,
or robin feathers resemble
tortoise shell, or my clam
has a closed heart.

Or why I confuse oregano with thyme,
stress relief doesn't always come
from my green pen,
or the scent of piñons.

I don't know why shadows
have more blue than gray,
vanilla is loved more often
than wintergreen, why
cerulean is a popular paint name,
and we forget to say it for the sky.

I don't know why sockeye
is named sockeye.

Or when I say a prayer
why I always think of what is woven.
Not a prickly pear, alone.

DESTINATION

The journey matters.
Pack the car your cat Phoebe

has never ridden in before.
Close her carrier while she cries

in oblong vowels for her velvet chair.
Tuck the amaryllis in the back seat,

not ivory like the one on the box,
soft as a lamb's ear. Instead it juts

star-like in a frisky baby red. Park
the Subaru in the jammed lot

at The Oasis, order Mahi-Mahi *bathed*
in heavy pepper cream. Enter the fragrant

shop and use your last cash to buy
your city friend a balsam light-ring

for her lamp, charge the Japanese
silk pillows painted in China for

your frugal mother; embroidered
fair-trade socks for your inhumane sister.

Ignore the terrible replica of a Navajo pot,
and the ridiculously expensive

essences of vervain, bergamot.
Drive through a million pines, watching

for black ice. Keep Phoebe in her carrier
until you open the door to the cabin,

then watch her gaze at the blue lighthouse
that blinks on your family's fridge,

and will continue to blink through all
the ripped tissues of Christmas.

Heavy Weather

in breathless hats,
in second-hand seas,

through windy labyrinths
of goopy news,

in colliding bagels,
and bleary olives,

over books half-gnawed
by cocker spaniels,

in aroused denim
and long-sleeved music,

with senior cranberries
and ageless teas,

in miraculous tales,
in marathon warnings,

in gaping gardens,
in the absent bees.

ON A BAD DAY

She cups a wild geranium's
tissue-paper blossoms,
their grains of soil,

their maps and shadows
burning with a scent
she knows.

She remembers bluebells
all over Ohio
where she roamed
with a friend, long gone,
and how bluebells
breathed on them,
as they foraged for morels
to sauté in basil and garlic.

She devours buttered toast
from the Hungarian
cobalt-blue dish
her cousin Norbert sent.

She remembers he lip-synced
Frank Sinatra songs for her
at his kitchen
table in Budapest.

She goes for a walk
among the junipers
of a ghost town,
and inches near a mine,

peering down its shaft,
wondering who would ever
lower themselves into that tiny
shadow of space.

COMING BACK

Take withered roots
like old flannel,
gray tea roses,
a broken honeycomb
to bury near the barn,

where hydrangea, still blue,
hangs from a beam
in a necklace of peppermint.

Touch the flowers,
the leaves, rustle
and crumble them,
smell tea, smell last summer.

Let the winter butter
of your right palm
grasp the shovel's
bitter handle,

and guide with your left
beyond the apple tree
in quarter-blossom.

Lift earth, its many worms,
turn the plot where mother-of-
thyme is somehow
never gone.

Come back to where
all the bees you wanted to hold
last fall, are moving shadows
at your elbows, little humming
nights bound with gold.

LAVENDER

I grow among the bitterness of brambles,
unholy desires of fireweed, the silver plan
of hornets. I grow among a gathering
of gladiolas, swelling crowns
of bee-balm, blushes
of the scentless, the psychoses
of roses. I feel the fevers
of lilies, peer inside the freckled throats
of foxgloves. I listen
to the impatience of asters,
the hum of milkweed, troubles
of the snowball flowers,
ginger syllables of zinnias. My loves
lean toward my evergreen, for what
I will remember. I will
remember.

CILANTRO

In my garden's abundant light,
cilantro lifts its flickering
scent of celery and mint.

Such gentle green spines
from tiny black seeds
he once hid under my pillow
in their elegant packet.

When I part the row
with my ankles,
fronds open their eyes,
their mouths.

Garden of cilantro in the desert!
Radiant in their bed—
ménage à trois of the tomato,
the onion, cilantro's carnal
teeth of tranquility.

And later, with leaves
on the cutting board,
I am dappled, sashaying
to an other-worldly sea,

I am the lemony pine
on a starved tongue.

When I mince them
into the turquoise bowl,
they tell the truth about
jewels of asparagus,
juices of bluestem grass,
the mazes of our long love.

New Year Poem

What nourishes the violets
before they tremble
open? What brushes
a burrowing snake,
the whittled secrets
on its tail? What kick
do we get from a pear
that balms us?
What is this tidy sienna
when we've requested
a fire-engine of geranium?
What sweeps the mountain
like a fickle sponge?
Who blames a circus of cirrus?
What is serious?
What beetle wanders
in this necklace?
What needs some
ochre in every ghost town?
What blossom balances
in a hollow ear?
What wrong tides
have loved us?
What moon
in the crabapple
has loved us?
What eye has held us?

THE STORY BEHIND THE DREAM

unpeels the yellow violet,
drops one scarred apricot,
etches gills on grief,
harbors a winter halo,
lavenders the bungalow,
flaps like a handkerchief,
cups the teaks of spring,
paddles in a bramble,
puzzles with a tentacle,
mirrors the birded sea,
coils in the cuckoo clock,
cools beneath the reef,
fingers the glow of coral,
salts every whorl.

GOD, IN THE GARDEN,

being the woman you are,
you should know
about the milk
in the mason jar,
the cream so thick at the top
from the little Jersey next door,

how a teaspoon
on your blueberries
will butter your stomach,
flutter in your tapioca
that begs for an infusion
of lavender, with a pinch
of mint on top.

You should know
about the handkerchiefs
of my great-grandmother
biting the dust
after years in the trunk.
I unfold them to sew
a chemise from all the lilacs
and wild roses she tucked
up her sleeve.

You should know you are
snout and tentacle,
a brazen hornet.
I am mad too.

You are a Northern Lights
beer and a plate of whitefish livers.
You are a tail dangling
from the willow,
a sweater of shaggy balloons,
and a bite of sassafras.

I look to your cedar fingernail
and your haloed cookie,

your grapefruit flea
and choppy engine,
your sleepy llama
and drizzle of rust,
your paddling syllables,
your fruit cellar full
of invisible jewels.

THE OLD TREE AND THE NEW TREE

a birthday poem

The old tree is pure white,
utterly fragrant.

When I walk between it
and the new tree,

I feel breaths from both of them
on my shoulders, my neck.

The new tree has smaller
blossoms, barely pink.

By afternoon
things are moving, the wind,
the bees.

For four days I love the blossoms
of the old tree and the new tree.

One will have apples,
the other crabapples.

I'll make my crimson jelly
from the old tree.

But this morning, the air is full of flowers.

CRABAPPLE TREE

You would have to know it was there,
white and breathless.

And then how alive
it is with tilting bees
living each light minute
of the day, drunk
and swaying through petals,
going in deep and whole.

Look up and through
the crossing layers
of snowy-looking boughs,
success without the weight
of snow, just like light and
the hum of something running,
someone who has sung.

Imagine how they'll sleep
as they shiver on this sweetness
all their lives, but still accept
the quickness, the cold.

It's not a long way off,
this end not really an end
but a way of going wholly
into our wings, into
the hearts of our bodies.

4. Notes to God from County Road H

DROUGHT

I think you are here
somewhere

where oceans of stars
once fell into orbit,

and rolled up on the shore
of the skies,

and grew where they
died and blew up,
seeding in gas
to make some new suns.

You could be the Space Roar,
the red swirl of Jupiter's Storm,
the Alien Star,
or that crab who lives on Mars.

~

This morning
I want to keep
the rosy light

that surfs
in the violet,

two flickers
of cream

that know what they will
become,

as the sky reels in
its cup of flowers,

and I walk out beneath,
beneath it all, in this skin

I bare, and love.

~

I watch the soft mouths
of range cows,
in the hot desert, eating the last
bale of alfalfa.

They are black,
so beautifully black,
breaths wet and green
as they sway toward
my empty hands.

I watch a pair of finches,
who follow me to where I wash
my hands, quiet finches,
good looking ones, who
flutter in my run-off.

I watch a horse
in my neighbor's small field,
the one I have brought a pear to,
all white with a half-moon
that cups her left eye.

She gets wild when the trailer comes.
She will ride to Nine-Mile Canyon
to live for the summer,
between sky and sage and juniper.

~

The poet loves texture
and wicked drama.

She wants the scent of sunrise
in cadmium yellow
on her paper.

She wants the blue hip
of a mountain,
the white-gold of a blossom,

the bee, the bee inside
the crystal
of a frozen tulip.

She believes in
the ancient furnace,
the bitter orange in the fridge.

She opens an envelope
to a small credit
that saves her.

The poet wants to hold
the first iris
inside the creek
of her heart.

She touches
a watercolor brush
and fears for the animal.

~

God, I remember praying
to you, you who were the father
of a son who was kinder.

~

You are a man
playing piano
with childish fingers.

~

I am a woman,
a robin, a tiger.

~

My friend
is so sick.
The chemo has been over
months ago.

Her day worships
the way she used to be.
A pianist, a poet,
she doesn't hear,
is dizzy when she stands,

eats the tofu
of lamplight, tofu
of coffee grounds,
of snow, of sky
long and promising.

My friend
jiggles a butterfly
pencil and opens
the wine of her writing,
the wine of cold tea.

She makes sure her dogs
are lean and happy,
running for the ball,
the special biscuit.

~

I love the husky notes
of the yellow-headed
blackbird,

this scout
here all day, fence
to spruce, his song

a cactus with shoulders,
sure as a mermaid's,
inside this ancient desert sea,

his gold hood
and coal body
like sun on Chicago.

He calls from my clothesline,
my red gate, my crabapple,
here to look for water

in our desert,
this body, this light,
this voice.

~

There are no answers
when I pray for more lemon balm,
less starlight,
a few straggly hollyhocks
through days of diamond-cutting heat.

What comes from the calls of magpies?
Two sprigs of dill
and one green hummingbird.

What swirls in my mug?
An ounce of dark chocolate.

I have finally put out sun tea.
I have lost the wild monkey-flower.

What days will not open?
Those inside the rodeos
of rainless clouds.

What happened to my windows?
They're etched with dust.

A bright yellow bee
lives one day on my screen,
and then dies holding on.

I have bought a delphinium
because I love the depth of its purple.

I will conserve dishwater, pee, spit,
to water it.

~

My neighbor says
What could be better
than beans
refried by someone else?

After my mother dies,
she whitens a scarf
my mother crocheted for me,
irons its stars wide open.

She knows I'm across
the street motherless,
fatherless.

She says she doesn't believe
in dinosaurs.

She buys me a bible.

She can't stand up
to roll tortillas anymore,
her knees given out.

Mornings she has the TV on
to Jimmy Swaggart.

She told me she grew up
in a pueblo and remembers
the scent of sage. I bring her
some from the desert,
and she smells with her eyes closed.

~

Who will remember the peace of aspen,
the gentle shine of scorpions?

The luck of sandstone?
The lope of a mesa?

The dinosaur footprint
in the heavens of a coal mine?

Who will remember
the troll of bootlace,
the hem of history,
an atrocity every day?

Who will remember the foot trail
through bramble and fireweed?

The next awkward step
full of fragrance?

Who will remember
the gypsy mushrooms,
the blink of sparrows,
the flames
of gambel oak?

The butter?

The brine?

~

I believe
there is nothing better
than an apricot blossom,

or my dog's white muzzle
nudging my wrist
to ask a question.

Nothing better
than a note that says
I'll be back
in an hour, my love...

Or this pen that floats an ore ship
inside its small blue capsule,

this pen that brings back
a walk in wild stones
between the Bears Ears;
or a trek on snowy miles
to find icy fireworks
in a Lake Superior cave.

Nothing better
than bumper stickers
May peace bewitch you
and *There is no mad tofu disease,*
my son just sent from his red
mailbox on Geranium Street,
in a priority envelope.

There is nothing more miraculous
than evolution right before
our eyes in the deep
Congo River where
the "elephant-fish"
can easily pick food
among river-pebbles
with its cylindrical mouth,

or a petroglyph panel
with a herd of deer,
and human figures
like bee-body
ghosts that float
on a sandstone wall
in Buckhorn Wash,

under the shine of desert varnish
where water slips over a cliff
in fingers of darkness.

~

Tonight, I am on the porch
under the snow
of the Milky Way.

I am far enough to believe
Venus is a sign of hope,
swaddled in its
greenhouse gases.

I keep a gray feather
as a bookmark,
my breath strips
and toe warmers,
a sponge my son
says can breed disease
in my kitchen.

I use an eraser in the shape of a butterfly,
the word I take apart to make
era, err, sere, erase.

On my desk, a Navajo woman
carved from sandstone
wears a nick at her shoulder,
her green rug full of my dust.

Tonight, I will make bean enchiladas
and doctor a can of adobo.
I will drink from the peach glass
etched in morning glories.

I've bought a lily, and sit next to it,
breathing its drift,
remembering lost Easters.

I am waiting this week
for the first Sacred Datura.

~

What wisdom in the curve
of a dog's paw,

in its descending
blossom,

its pads that need earth,
its run that forgets balance,
its transcendence towards us.

Aren't we
moving towards happiness
always, moving aside

the shells and the orange peels,
the tin cans and chamomile,

moving aside the bills
we have torn, and finally
paid up?

~

My dog is brown
with a white triangle
at his throat.

He sleeps under
green fleece,

with an ancient sense
that knows *burrow*,

ears that have to believe
in silence.

He is unafraid
when he sees a dagger
of lightning,

feels a world of thunder
in his heart.

STAR ROUTE

I find a dead bear,
whole, limp, hit by a car
in the middle of the road home.

It's a yearling, and its darkness
makes me think of life
where there were no stars.

~

Tonight the moon looks like a claw.

Orion is blurred by a wisp,
but I still try to trace
his waist.

~

I keep thinking I will vaporize
into balance,

breathe so well I am always
in the present.

My body will not let go
of the other worlds
I have lived through

in its unlit rooms
of mauve, plum, periwinkle,
or maybe an organ
green with the life
of decay.

~

I am tired of how hunters
bait bears with garbage,
train dogs to tree them,
the bears' hunger like mine,

their snouts a terrible miracle,
their bodies
a prize.

~

My body will not let go
of imagining the routines
of those I know and love,
good friends, my niece,
their days of paradise

in a hand-blown glass pipe,
or nightly fifths, their
prayers to you, their
love of death,

the hurt
in the body's center
melting into
all the mercurial colors of love.

~

Where are the lost stars?

Daughters and sons looking for sweetness.

We have come through
these waters,
these stories,
to this:

after millions of years
we are ready to live
in another galaxy.

~

The Rochester Panel
mazed with ancient petroglyphs
off my windswept Utah highway
up a canyon jittered with upheavals,

on the rock's red varnish,
hundreds of figures are etched,
opening their bodies to one another
in sex and birth,
surrounded by snakes, deer, goats,
shields and spears.

The humans have big eyes
and large heads.
Maybe aliens, my friend joked.
She went there in high school
to breathe near this news,
to be taken away
by these lives persisting
in stone for a thousand years.

They will always
be a half-mystery,
except for the women
looking up from childbirth
to what lives
behind the sky.

ABOUT THE AUTHOR

Nancy Takacs's poetry awards include The Juniper Prize, the 2018 and 2016 *15 Bytes* Book Award for Poetry, Weber's Sherwin W. Howard Award, a 2020 Pushcart Prize, and a runner-up for the *Missouri Review* Editor's Prize. She is the author of three other books of poetry and four chapbooks. Nancy lives most of the year in the high-desert town of Wellington, Utah, and spends time in Bayfield, Wisconsin, near the Apostle Islands National Lakeshore, in a small cabin with her husband, poet Jan Minich. Their son Ian Minich is a photographer in Salt Lake City. Nancy is the inaugural Poet Laureate of Utah's art hub: Helper City.

Recent Titles from Mayapple Press

Zilka Joseph, *In Our Beautiful Bones,* 2021
    Paper, 108pp, $19.95 plus s&h
    ISBN: 9780-1-952781-07-0
Ricardo Jesús Mejías Hernández, tr. Don Cellini, *Libro de Percances/*
Book of Mishaps, 2021
    Paper, 56pp, $18.95 plus s&h
    ISBN: 978-952781-05-6
Eleanor Lerman, *Watkins Glen,* 2021
    Paper, 218pp, $22.95 plus s&h
    ISBN: 978-1-952781-01-8
Betsy Johnson, *when animals are animals,* 2021
    Paper, 58pp, $17.95 plus s&h
    ISBN: 978-1-952781-02-5
Jennifer Anne Moses, *The Man Who Loved His Wife,* 2021
    Paper, 172pp, $20.95 plus s&h
    ISBN: 978-1-936419-96-8
Judith Kunst, *The Way Through,* 2020
    Paper, 76pp, $17.95 plus s&h
    ISBN: 978-1-936419-98-2
Ellen Stone, *What Is in the Blood,* 2020
    Paper, 72pp, $17.95 plus s&h
    ISBN 978-1-936419-95-1
Terry Blackhawk, *One Less River,* 2019
    Paper, 78pp, $16.95 plus s&h
    ISBN 978-1-936419-89-0
Ellen Cole, *Notes from the Dry Country,* 2019
    Paper, 88pp, $16.95 plus s&h
    ISBN 978-1-936419-87-6
Monica Wendel, *English Kills and other poems,* 2018
    Paper, 70pp, $15.95 plus s&h
    ISBN 978-1-936419-84-5
Charles Rafferty, *Something an Atheist Might*
Bring Up at a Cocktail Party, 2018
    Paper, 40pp, $14.95 plus s&h
    ISBN 978-1-936419-83-8

For a complete catalog of Mayapple Press publications, please visit our website at *www.mayapplepress.com*. Books can be ordered direct from our website with secure on-line payment using PayPal, or by mail (check or money order). Or order through your local bookseller.